The Surveyors

The Surveyors

POEMS BY

Mary Jo Salter

Alfred A. Knopf · New York · 2017

THIS IS A BORZOI BOOK
PUBLISHED BY ALFRED A. KNOPF

Copyright © 2017 by Mary Jo Salter

www.aaknopf.com

Knopf, Borzoi Books, and the colophon are registered trademarks of
Penguin Random House LLC.

Library of Congress Cataloging-in-Publication Data

Names: Salter, Mary Jo., author.
Title: The surveyors : poems / by Mary Jo Salter.
Description: First Edition. | New York : Alfred A. Knopf, 2017.
Identifiers: LCCN 2016042321 (print) | LCCN 2016048870 (ebook) |
     ISBN 9781524732660 (hardcover)| ISBN 9781524732677 (ebook)
Classification: LCC PS3569.A46224 A6 2017 (print) | LCC PS3569.
     A46224 (ebook) | DDC 811/.54—dc23
LC record available at https://lccn.loc.gov/2016042321

Jacket photography by Oote Boe
Jacket design by Chip Kidd

Manufactured in the United States of America
First Edition

for Keith

Contents

IV.

I

YIELD

That's what the sign said
below my window.
I'd step out of bed

to look down on the fork
the Y had made
in the word and the road.

YIELD was destined
for a field of YELLOW,
but scrambled like eggs

into something like DAILY.
Was firm, was an order,
but just meant CONSIDER.

And consider I did.
I stared at the sign
that was so little needed:

to stay or to go?
That was for others,
my parents, to know.

He might leave someday.
She might stay behind.
I was only one side

of the triangle.
I'd slip back in bed,
back into my own mind,

and more letters wanting
to play came to me
alone to untangle.

BRATISLAVA

So I'm still alive and now I'm in Bratislava.
That's funny. I hadn't expected to be alive.

A sign in italics nudges us at the station:
Have an amazing time in Bratislava!

That's funny: a straight-faced wish, offered in English
and then Slovakian, posted above a trash can

that stands like the only monument in town.
We've heard there's a castle, though. We need a tram.

We take one, and it heads in the wrong direction.
A pretty girl, cheerful and blond, straightens us out,

and we get on and off a bus at the proper stops.
That's funny. Already a right place and a wrong one

to be in Bratislava, and I am among
the people who sort of get this, at least at the moment

I happen to occupy, within a vacation
in Vienna with a day trip to Bratislava.

That's funny. I'd assumed my travel companion
through life would be my husband, even if

I'd gone to Bratislava, which I hadn't thought of
long enough to think I would or wouldn't.

The spanking white castle, standing high on a hill
we climb on foot, swigging our bottles of Coke,

dates to the year 800 or so, but burned
down to the ground, which tends, as we know, to happen,

and was reconceived in one of the worst times of all,
the 1950s, under Soviet rule.

That's funny. Atop embarrassing pillars, knights
in plaster armor gaze up at the sky

triumphantly, although what for is forgotten,
and the sunlight they eclipse in silhouette

is all the sillier on those phallic cannons
between their legs, with three or four cannonballs.

More cannonballs per man. That's human history
in a nutshell. Bullies unsated with all they've got

and below, the blindsided masses. That's what it is.
And yet I'm happy, now, with my companion—

he likes me, I like him. He has his own backstory
of bleak encampments, battles lost, and sorrows

best not spoken of in Bratislava
lest we spoil our day, which so far is duly amazing.

I admire his dignity. Dignity is funny.
Everything's funny now, which we hadn't expected

to happen, either of us, after what happened.
We're still alive and now we're in Bratislava.

THE PROFANE PIANO TUNER

I finally let him go,
the man who'd tune our innocent piano
twice a year or so.

He knew his stuff,
and for a while, that was enough:

I'd leave the room so he could hit
B flat again and shout, *You little shit,*
Come on, you bastard, pounding and pounding it.

Hour after hour he'd swear
You filthy whore, Oh don't you dare,

you stinking, stupid bitch—
a litany of abuses which
he couldn't hear, though blessed with perfect pitch.

One day I understood.
Why pretend I'd tuned him out? What good

could come from smiling through profanities
like black, ill-tempered keys
against the white—black rage in twos and threes?

He said when he was done:
A perfect day! Hey look, we've got some sun.

I answered *We're in luck!*
and handed him his check and watched his truck
back out the driveway, thinking *You dumb fuck,*

not knowing I would think that. Very strange.
My daughter, who'd been out of range

all day at school,
sailed in and sat down, lifted up her profile,
and played a Chopin prelude like an angel.

PASTRY LEVEL

I was gazing out back
at the lemon-gold
sun on the cream-colored painted brick
of the new house.

(New again, I mean.
I've told you the story—
that it was finished just a few
months shy of the war;

that young families
moved in and out before a widow
who couldn't care for it anymore
signed it over to me,

a single buyer lately
possessed by self-
possession.) This morning
at my writing table, looking

outward for a word,
in that sun-glaze on the wall
I saw again a baker's shelf
twenty years ago in Paris.

You were there, of course.
The average American
four-year-old girl
stands at forty inches tall,

if you can get her
to stand still.
When you were four,
in those ruffled French dresses

I couldn't help spending
a fortune on,
you couldn't be kept away
from patisserie

after patisserie;
you guided me by the hand
to every window display
that we might inspect another batch

of little pleated
tartes au citron,
glistening neatly
at the level of your eye.

Remember when
you, your sister,
your father and I
all spoke the same language?

Because of you
we invented a phrase—
"pastry level"—
to indicate the height of any

four-year-old on the street . . .
It seemed to go without saying
we'd be strolling together
all the rest of our days.

ALOE

Somewhere between the store
where I'd bought the aloe plant
and its home arrival,

one waxen, prickly spear
had been rent in half.
Why leave a dead thing dangling

by a string? I snapped it off.
A pearly unguent oozed
into my palm, as if

I were the one bruised.
Well, if it thought so, sure.
I rubbed it in my skin.

So rough: I hadn't taken
care in so long . . . And why
hadn't I cried for help?

In the morning, a fresh ally
by instinct with itself,
the aloe had sealed up

its broken fingertip—
a low, but unbowed beauty
in its handicap.

My hand, not soft, was softer.
Well then, healing aloe?
Something to allow?

MR. BOYFRIEND

New lover, known and unknown,
you've risen before dawn
and, delicious in suit and tie,
you lean down to the bed
to kiss my rumpled head
the tenderest goodbye.

A military bearing
adheres to what you're wearing.
Oh, how many years
did I wait to know a man
who knows he is a man
and not a boy?—who steers

himself through the long day
and rides it, come what may,
in a waft of aftershave
and the bracing, scratchy starch
of his dress shirt? As you march
off to the office, brave

and clear-eyed in your tortoise-
shell glasses, looking gorgeous,
I feel both safe and weak
slipping back to your kiss
in my sleep, and the light graze
of your cuff link on my cheek.

DRAGNET

The story you are about to read is true.
The names have been changed to protect the internet.

I'm thinking back to that old show, *Dragnet*,
starring Jack Webb, before the World Wide Web

was possible. I'm thinking about the "data dragnet"
the talking heads have been talking about

on TV today. There was congressional oversight.
There was bipartisan agreement

and I have an alibi. I was at home
when it happened. When I turned on my laptop,

when I answered my phone. OK, I admit it,
I wasn't at home, not right then, not that minute,

but there's bicameral oversight
over my sidewalk, and both of their videos

confirm I was only taking out the trash,
even if nothing now is the trash,

it's all permanent, but here's the good news,
we're training young people, but never enough,

in computer science to sift through the stuff
we thought we deleted, and meanwhile we're all

going to live longer and longer, thanks
to advances in medicine, and the universe

will go on expanding and we'll be so advanced
in years that all that we say will be gibberish.

I just thought of something unnerving, though.
Your robot will know you—a robot who sounds

just like Jack Webb. What a terrible actor.
I don't mean robot, I mean avatar,

your cyborg twin, your remotely piloted
vehicle, your 3-D sort-of friend

who will never be bored by who you are
or by what you don't understand.

TODAY'S SPECIALS

Why did I come tonight?
Too late: I've handed my keys
to some boy valet, polite

to the point of insolence.
He's so young, I'm so old—
really, why take offense

or even take the time,
the precious time, to reflect
that I was once like him,

appalled at the parade
of the hair-sprayed and the bald?
I tip him, scan the crowd,

and advance toward the cliques
of nerds, cheerleaders, potheads,
jocks, and Jesus freaks

I'd felt awkward with, and forty
years on, at last are peers:
yes, this is my party.

It's mid-June, and bright tents
are erected to shield our kind
against the elements,

which hardly could be milder.
A faint breeze stirs the scents
of sunscreen, crab cakes, beer,

cut grass, and gasoline.
I think I'll get a drink.
I begin to cross the lawn

(ducking that guy I dated
once or twice, and did he
see me? Do I seem . . . dated?)

and spot, beside the wine bar,
a whiteboard with *Today's
Specials* in black marker.

Why do I trust my eyes?
I can't read at this distance.
I'm nearer now—and surprise,

here's what it really says:
In Memoriam. What
genius arranged for this?

How thoughtful and horrible.
Different hands have come
as they once did at school

to diagram the sentence
of those who left us first.
More like taking attendance:

names, dates, an excuse
for absence when it's known—
cancer, accident. Who's

that, Bob Rogers? Bob.
My funny, uncle-faced pal,
pride of the Drama Club,

who tended to land the role
of banker or judge because
he had a middle-aged middle?

Dead at thirty-seven.
He probably looked the same
as he had at seventeen,

while most of us lived to stare
for decades at the stage
makeup in the mirror

that gave back our true age.
Bob Rogers. I played your kid.
Our names met on a page

in playbills kept awhile,
tossed away—just as I turn
now from the other special

names for today, and scout
for anyone to talk with
to drive the wisdom out.

A WORD FROM OUR SPONSOR

Tell me it is not a work of art,
the one where the little boy in the backseat of his father's car
looks up at a rocket being fired from the desert out into space,
all combustion and speed
while he remains only a little boy, and he says simply, softly,
"Whoa,"
a drawn-out "whoa," as you might say to a horse.

Meanwhile, the rocket keeps going up,
and the astronaut, viewed at a thrilling, almost vertical angle
as he climbs the sky with his astronaut buddy,
looks down at the ever-tinier car traversing the empty landscape,
the really cool car the astronaut envies
from the vehicle he is now propelled in
but cannot steer, any more than the boy can—
no, neither of them gets to drive—
and looking down at the car, the astronaut says simply, softly,
"Whoa."

These are the two words written by the ad man—
"Whoa" and "Whoa"—and you might look down on him
as being so much smaller than the poet,
though his paycheck is larger;
you might call the poet more sophisticated;
but just *you* try to do it, try to say something symmetrical
and yet so unexpected.

If I were a cultural critic, now
would be the time to claim that this commercial
is a thirty-second hymn to imperialism,
to the astronaut's arrogation of the air, and the boy's
father's conquering of the wide-open American spaces,
that it's a hymn to masculine muscle, to boundless
consumption, to wanting and wanting despite

our having so much, but the truth is
that although I've seen this ad a dozen times now
and vow to memorize the Mercedes, the BMW, whatever it is,
I never recall the make of the car
or even its color.

All I remember is how very efficient
the commercial is, as elegant as an engine,
how gently funny, how affectionate its gesture at the human
manufacture of wonder, and I reflect
that the artist is one who sometimes commands the courage
to pare everything down to two iterations
of one word that cannot be translated.

WE'LL ALWAYS HAVE PARENTS

It isn't what he said in *Casablanca*
and it isn't strictly true. Nonetheless
we'll always have them, much as we have Paris.
They're in our baggage, or perhaps *are* baggage
of the old-fashioned type, before the wheels,
which we remember when we pack for Paris.
Or don't remember. Paris doesn't know
if you're thinking of it. Neither do your parents,
although they say you ought to visit more,
as if they were as interesting as Paris.
Both Paris and your parents are as dead
and as alive as what's inside your head.
Meanwhile, those lovers, younger every year
(because with every rerun we get older),
persuade us less, for all their cigarettes
and shining unshed tears about the joy
of Paris blurring in their rearview mirror,
that they've surpassed us in sophistication.
Granted, they were born before our parents
but don't they seem by now, Bogart and Bergman,
like our own children? Think how we could help!
We could ban their late nights, keep them home
the whole time, and prevent their ill-starred romance!
Here's looking at us, Kid. You'll thank your parents.

VIERGE OUVRANTE

Marvelous and a little sick
that her immaculate ivory
self is sawn into a triptych

from her uncrowned head straight down
the neck, the breastbone, and the lap
enthroning her bisected son.

Magnetic on the double-door
refrigerator of her white
body, he is miniature

but mature, an all-suffering
king already killed, reborn,
who elevates one hand in blessing

while the other must hold steady
the great globe on his knee, the whole
world that is his baby—

or will be when the world's redeemed.
But this is France, the year 1200,
and to the sculptor it has seemed

both beautiful and necessary
that the hinged, compliant Virgin
unfold the living allegory

buried in her anatomy,
as if some holy madman surgeon
scarified there, in the three

small panels, the naked guts of sin
coiled and twisting in the back-
story of the coming Passion:

instead of one loved child who grows
within her, here are multiple
horror shows, the Man of Sorrows

mocked along his bitter path,
the stations of the Cross that lead
to the death she's pregnant with.

Come the French Revolution, she
too will be a thing of scorn.
Turned into a children's toy

fitted with four wheels and a cord
to pull around the Queen of Heaven,
what to do but be drawn forward

to Baltimore, where now, a vision
butterflied on her stand, she's propped
up like the one Book's one edition?

She knows the future is past mending.
Why look to her for an opening
for some other ending?

THE BICKERS

It's as if he's edible
himself, the overfed young man
clutching a greenish pair of gloves
like a bunch of steamed asparagus.
His wavy hair is chestnut. His face
is packed with juice, a pale pink cherry
topping the pudding of his body,
or topping what tops it first, the white
dollop of a scalloped collar.
His velvet cloak is a salmon color.
Even the golden frame that hems
him in is delicious, its baroque
buttercreams of ornament
the slathered icing on the cake.

His counterpart, a perfect match
(at least by the measure of the canvas
and the same resplendent frame),
hangs just to his left. How strange
I'd walked past without noticing.
The painter's skill is just as fine:
that lifelike treatment of the hand
holding a small, improving book;
the black shape of the suit set off
by a paper-white, fine-pleated ruff
and a bearded, balding head. A man
who's prosperous but moderate,
diligent and slightly peeved—
the languid young man's father, surely.

Bartholomeus van der Helst
painted them both, I'm reading now,
in 1642. They were
the famous Bickers of Amsterdam.
The Bickers! Savor too the name.
Picture the Bickers' League, a band
of seven family politicians
holding office all at once.
Andries, the father here, was mayor
time and again, a mercantile
diplomat who sought to make
the world safe for his shipping routes.
Thanks to pragmatists like him,
the Eighty Years' War stopped at last.

That was a topic van der Helst
would paint too, as a grand tableau:
*Banquet at the Crossbowmen's Guild
in Celebration of the Treaty
of Munster*. Here the revelers are,
deaf to whatever caused the war,
shaking hands and doffing hats,
lifting refilled pilsner glasses,
and letting their long hose fall down
into their floppy, wide-cut boots.
Poor Andries, meanwhile—stuck
beside that spoiled brat on the wall,
his only child, Gerard, who ate
the fruits of other people's work!

Opposites attract, and yet
one Bicker only can endure
at the Rijksmuseum gift shop
as a refrigerator magnet.
Gerard, of course. Who'd want his dad,
that pious trading magnate, for
a souvenir of all that's sour?
It hardly matters he had cause.
The old war of the generations
outlives all truces, and remains
rich fodder for our snickering.
Taking a seat at the café,
I order waffles with whipped cream
and can hear the Bickers, bickering.

LITTLE MEN

Two men I've loved loved little men
when they were little children—
tin soldiers they could push around
the carpet in their little fists.
They could play all antagonists,

make sound effects for every sound,
but were peremptory and unfair
as those Olympian puppeteer
gods in the *Iliad*. All alone
each boy beat the odds and won.

And stunned the enemy the next day
from some new flank, and changed which war
it was, and pretended uniforms
were colors other than they were.
And rarely put the toys away

because war is eternal.
(Myself, I'd had a paper doll
I dressed, and dressed, and dressed to kill.)
Of these two boys who ordered all
the playroom into battle, one

grew up to be a novelist.
Reader, I married him; we lost.
The other rose in rank to Colonel,
draft-numbered for a distant war
nobody wanted anymore,

and nobody is more pacifist.
We read the daily news in bed,
updates to the casualty list
that verifies more little men
have won, and winning's what to have.

And me? Which side should I be on?
Hope too is eternal.
I'm on his side, beside my love:
the story rests here with my head
against the drumbeat in his chest.

SMOKING THE DEAD SEA SCROLLS

A flickering black-and-white
documentary reel
recalls them at their feast:

long tables spread with fragments
in Aramaic and Hebrew,
with tags in Arabic

numerals like place cards
for scholars in white shirts.
It's 1952,

five years since Bedouin
shepherds broke a pot
in a cave; and in their lab

the puzzle-solvers laugh
at something, with a silent-
movie hamminess.

"Turn this way." (You imagine
the voice of the cameraman.)
One of them looks up

from a snippet of Scotch tape
he's affixing to a scrap
of antiquity (the next

generation's task
will be, we know, to scrape
a yellow gum from the text),

while the sun—the very sun
of Creation—illuminates
through flung-open windows

the crumbling manuscripts
darkness kept legible
over millennia.

The young man resumes his work,
pressing a curled parchment
flat with one hand, and raising

with the other hand his half-
finished cigarette,
a tiny, perfect scroll

of paper that burns his lungs
pleasantly, as an era
is vanishing in smoke.

ST. FLORIAN WITH BURNING CHURCH

Funny how you can pass time and again
the same things in the same room and not see them.
Somehow, pacing for years through this museum,
I've slighted three-foot-high St. Florian
and now I stop. Why now? Saint who? Consult
smartphone: apparently, he was a cult

figure, often featured with a pail
of water like this, ever tipped to douse
the flames engulfing, at his feet, a house—
no, it's a church, but to a dollhouse-scale.
Medieval artists played with small and large:
the point here is that Florian took charge.

His pose is wooden; then again, he's made
(as is the water and the fire) of wood
and everything about them is a falsehood.
"Light a fire," the legend says he said,
"and I will climb to Heaven on it." One
comment like that, your bio is all done—

a millennium passes and the fire motif
has gotten out of hand; a Roman soldier
martyred in 304 C.E., now you're
a fetish throughout Europe, and (good grief)
credited with extinguishing whole towns.
In real life, though, it's Florian who drowns

and sinks to the bottom, poor unread footnote.
They club him, scourge and flay him; for good measure,
they throw him in the Enns, the local river,
a millstone dangling from his soft young throat.
Later, a woman named Valeria takes
his body from the deep: and thus his relics

travel through Noricum (in present-day
Austria), to Linz, then Cracow, where
the church named after him commands the square.
Today in Poland, all you have to say
is "Florian!" on the phone: it's understood
as code, even now, to call the fire brigade.

Submission is the mark of all the saints,
too humble to protest how history paints
their acts in its canonical report.
As for the rest of us, who knows our sins?
Some vague, antique offense occurred near Linz,
famous for Hitler and the Linzertorte.

ADVANTAGE FEDERER

The Holy Roman Empire comes to mind
tonight, as I sit among the nineteen thousand
in Madison Square Garden, which is not
anywhere near Madison, nor is it square,
nor is it a garden.

Still, even Voltaire
could have found something holy about it,
partly because the real Placido Domingo
is in the stands, enduring the microphone
somebody jams in his face on the Jumbotron;

and also because, loud as opera, in a cloud
of dry ice from the locker room pit,
a herald's voice proclaims that it is Fed
himself parting the crowd, and by god that's him,
the Greatest of All Time.

His opponent gets some hoopla, but how can he rate?
I scrutinize Roger's legs (shapely and human,
in shorts trimmed by a gold tuxedo stripe)
with the same imploring attention I've seen him train
on the face of his racket

in close-ups on TV; and look, he's doing it now,
plucking pensively at the Wilson logo,
the W in the mirror: *I am the man,
I can do this*. All the chanters agree he can:
let's go, Roger, let's go!

And yet . . . although our tickets buy us space,
time is an ace; the match is whizzing by.
First set, second, third. Now he has lost.
Now all the talking, graying heads can say
into their cameras gravely: How long can he last?

Oh but elation has the highest ranking!
Surely I'm winning, simply by being alive
while Roger Federer is thirty-three
and playing like an angel and also blessing
the sponsors and the "Baby Fed" Dimitrov:

"I'd like to thank Grigor for beating me."
Seventh Avenue is seventh heaven
as I float out into the evening, hardly aware
of the rain when I open my umbrella's face
to stare into it, as Federer might stare.

TENNIS IN THE SNOW

You looked up from your book, and apropos
of nothing, asked: Did I ever tell you
I played tennis once in the snow?

No, I said. You didn't. Where was this?

Tennis in the snow! you said again.
It was . . . in Colorado. No, in Kansas.
I was a young captain.

Did you win?

I don't know. I'd play this guy at the base.
Marty. I can see us laughing,
slipping and sliding all over the place.

Were tennis balls still white back then?

(A smile from you.) No, they were yellow
already. This was the late eighties.
It wasn't all *that* long ago.

❄

Oh, I said. That's a shame.
I'm picturing the big white flakes
whirling around, and part of the game

was that you guys could hardly tell
the difference between falling snow
and the big white fuzzy tennis ball

or even the full moon that would seem
to lob over your heads that night,
like a movie or a dream.

It was daytime, you said. Nice story, though.

Sorry, I said. I should leave it there.
I just wanted to be mixed up in it,
the place where your memories are.

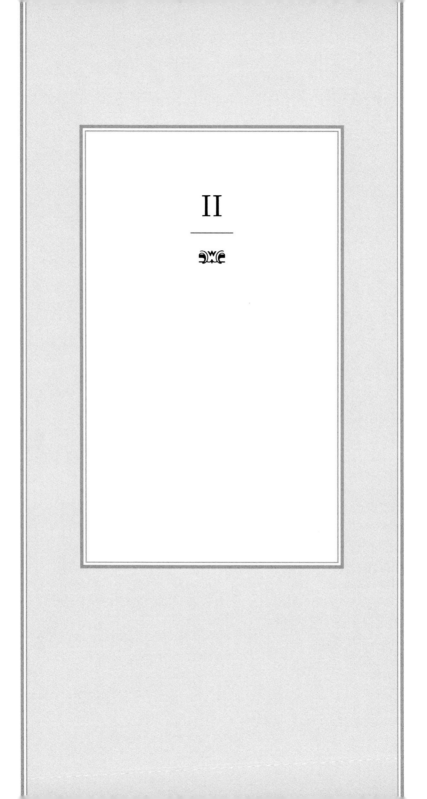

II

THE SURVEYORS

*Also, I had a dream, about a year and half ago, that I read a poem
called "The Surveyors," and it was by you. Does this poem exist?
I cannot remember any of the words, only that there were all four
seasons in it, and that there were nice descriptions of a chain being
made taut, the running out of the chain, over and over . . .*

for Matthew Yeager, who wrote me this letter

Dear Matt,
I'm sorry to say "The Surveyors" does not exist,
despite my being haunted by your question
for a long while now, imagining time and again
that the past can change; that the poem is on the list
of things I did once, because you dreamed it of me.
It's true, I regret, I've never put all four
seasons into one poem, though the Shakespeare
sonnet I love most keenly, 73
("That time of year thou may'st in me behold"),
implies them, and I wish I'd made a gesture
at least of homage. But when I read your letter
in the autumn of my life, I felt no cold;
I heard Vivaldi's "Spring" scrape violins
over and over, like the running out of chains.

"Over and over, like the running out of chains"—
I've already quoted wrong the thing you said,
not being you. I can't be in your head.
You can't follow me back there, hearing strains
of Vivaldi in cafés. America
had just learned *cappuccino,* and to say
croissant, not *Danish;* we went for those parfait
glasses of yogurt, with strata of granola.
I was so new. The year was '73
or maybe '72. It doesn't matter.
I had discovered sex and poetry.
Thinking of either one would make me shudder.
I was happy. I was nervous about exams.
I was going to read all the works of Henry James.

I was going to read all the works of Henry James,
but haven't. So much unfinished business
unless you're Henry James, who had time to witness
every minute of life, then record the whole, it seems.
Yes, it was thrilling art, but also bad
to make us wait so long to locate Chad
and Madame de Thing in their adulterous boat.
The Europeans or *The Ambassadors*—
the grandeur James could pour into a title!
That plural but hawk-like wisdom, above it all—
implied too by your title "The Surveyors."
Tripod and hard hat, compass, orange vest:
sometimes, I think, more grounded work is best,
or better than the poem you thought I wrote.

Or better than the poem you thought I wrote
is another one I never wrote: it's set
in shabby, hipster Zagreb, where my love
and I, now sixty, walked past shuttered shops
on a Sunday morning, and found ourselves in front of
the—really?—Museum of Broken Relationships,
which was open. Of course it was open. So we spent
time in the gift shop, where they charged the equivalent
of thirteen dollars for a little pink
eraser that would help you not to think.
RUB IT ALL OUT, it said. A pillowcase
read SLEEP IT OFF. By this age, I'd erased
much of my past quite nicely; so had he.
We walked out holding hands, a bit brokenly.

We walked out holding hands, a bit brokenly,
like Adam and Eve, in my favorite poem of all.
Milton! Thou shouldst be living at this hour
but you're not, since these two made sure you were mortal.
No human, though, can dream beyond the power
of your blind omniscience; modernity
in poetry must die if you don't last.
What's more Einsteinian than Book Eleven,
Michael escorting Adam up that hill
to make their space-time survey of the past
ahead, witnessed not just in the brain
but in present action? Cain killing Abel
as the seed of countless long-dead wars, and even
while Eve has not yet given birth in pain . . .

While Eve has not yet given birth in pain,
I have. I try to sneak a look, like Thetis,
over the shoulder of whatever may
now forge my daughters' prospects. Surely Auden
had Milton's scene in mind when he shaped his;
what Homer saw on his word-hammered shield
had taken on the sheen of the word-field
surveyed by Adam; implied an unnamed Mary,
who knew *It is written,* and that she must yield.
I live for nothing more than for my children,
yet I'll confess, Matt, I know well the If
Clause of self-sabotage: *If I must lose
my life, why not make this my hour to choose?*
Jesus, tempted, might have jumped off the cliff.

Jesus, tempted, might have jumped. Off the cliff
is where this-poem-that-isn't now must go.
Today in the paper ("the paper" has a whiff
of yesterday to it, sorry), Elon Musk
averred we might be living in a vast
computer simulation of a past
world re-created by our own descendants.
To them our metaphors can make no sense—
the summer of my life, my day at dusk . . .
Death, thou shalt die, said Donne. Could that be so?
The only instinct greater than survival
is, apparently, its keenest rival,
the drive to guarantee no thing's not dead.
Melt all the ice caps. Cut off every head.

Melt all the ice caps. Cut off every head
to serve the crude medieval god up there
and post the act on social media, where
all life went anyway—into the Cloud.
Numberless universes at this minute
(though what's a minute?) may be simulcast,
we're also told, in which case nothing's lost,
yet something's deathly in the infinite:
it leaves us mortals out. What's with this glee
we humans feel, enabling the posthuman?
Doubtless we'll come to singularity
with our machines, but why must we be glad?
A life from here to there, in one direction—
oh, I was content with what I had.

Oh, I was content with what I had:
a perch on the back stoop. I'm maybe three.
This is it, Matt, my first memory.
I'm in a wool coat, tailored, double-breasted,
absurd for a toddler; but that's how things were.
The president was Dwight D. Eisenhower.
So long ago! I look down from my great
height, the fourth step of new-poured concrete,
to survey the new sod of our new backyard.
My mother is on her knees. She's working hard,
making a garden, planting flowers between
different-sized rocks. She calls it a "rock garden."
Here in Grand Rapids, people are not so grand.
My mother is making art from her plot of dirt,

Japanese art, and the neighbors won't understand.
She'll spend a lot of time feeling proud and hurt.

She'll spend a lot of time feeling proud and hurt
like her daughter. I came by it honestly,
being stung by life, soothing myself with art,
making stuff up, getting things different-sized.
You doubt my first memory? I'm not surprised.
I must have fused two scenes, since nobody,
I see now, wears a winter coat in weather
warm enough to plant flowers in. It's wrong
and the sonnet I just wrote contained sixteen
lines, which even I know is too long.
I've lived already longer than my mother
and haven't lived enough. *Live all you can,*
said Lambert Strether; *it's a mistake not to.*
Living by this is the best I think I'll do.

Living by this is the best I think I'll do,
while praying not to burden those I love.
What hope I won't? When my time comes to vault
off the bridge, I'll be a midget, bent and frail
(I'm too short, even now, to clear the rail)
and besides (will they concede it's not my fault
my brain is shot?), I won't be good for new
information, or even old stuff I believe
nobody told me. Half-deaf, paranoid
nihilist nonsense, technophobic rants,
the imagined feats of grandchildren, the round

of half-true stories run into the ground—
and gone will be Vivaldi, sex, romance,
sweet things I must remember I've enjoyed.

Sweet things. I must remember. I've enjoyed
forgetting, then remembering again,
the running out (remember, Matt, the chain
gone taut, then running out, over and over?)
of what my life is, before it meets the void.
A buried marriage. Late, my truest lover.
My children jumping too high on the bed,
landing on college campuses. Goodbye,
goodbye, walk through that gate, don't watch me cry.
Lost friends, a dozen places I called home.
I can't see all I'm seeing—give me time!
If I wrote the poem you dreamed, would that imply
we'd finalized my list? . . . For now that's why,
I'm sorry to say, "The Surveyors" does not exist.

III

꧁꧂

from
Rooms of Light:
The Life of Photographs

Selected lyrics from a song cycle

Music by Fred Hersch
World Premiere, October 15, 2015
Kasser Theater
Montclair, New Jersey

PAPARAZZI

I wish I could escape the paparazzi!
They pop up everywhere I want to go.
I cannot shop, I cannot sunbathe topless,
I fly to Greece, I'm spied at the Acropolis.
   How did anyone know?

I wish I could escape the paparazzi!
They leap from limos like it's some big game—
At home they crouch for hours in my bushes.
I watch them lie in wait on their big tushes!
   Don't they have any shame?

I won a Golden Globe (OK, a nomination)—
but they were asking, was my stomach flat?
Did I look pregnant? Who might be the father?
Is he a rock star—if not, why bother?
   How shallow, to care about that!

I'm really shy, I am a private person.
Nobody knows how deep I am inside!
Yes, I love Gaultier, I'm wearing Prada,
but I'm happy in jeans, or nada.
   Where can a simple girl hide?

I wish I could escape the paparazzi!
If I could wave a magic wand today,
I would get rid of them in such a hurry!
I ought to sue them, then again I worry—
   what if they went away?

HERE I AM

Here I am, making my grand tour
the summer after graduation.
What is this? Must be the Rome train station.
We never noticed we were poor.
Backpacks and low-rise jeans—
we never lived beyond our means.
(Back then there were no ATMs.)
Here we are,
my friends and me.
We're napping on a bank of the Thames,
when love was free.

Here I am with that girl I met
on the trip to Brussels or Bruges.
(My God, her duffel bag is huge!)
What was her name? Yvonne? Yvette?
She ditched me; I'm forgetting why.
Oh yeah—when I slept with that Swedish guy.
His sleeping bag was full of fleas.
Here we are,
with our bread and cheese,
on a park bench in the Tuileries,
when love was free.

Here I am,
a woman in the middle
of her life,
and her life
is an endless riddle.

In all of Europe
I couldn't stir up
a memory more un-
likely and foreign
than me at twenty-two.
I can't help gazing
at her bright young eyes,
at her nice firm thighs.
Was I ever twenty-two?
Look at her skin, it's amazing.
Can you be me? Am I you?

Here I am at the Berlin Wall.
They tore it down, but it's still there
in this picture, like my long dark hair.
But there's a wall between her and me
that, like me, won't be getting thinner.
Here we are,
myself and me,
thinking, *Ich bin ein Berliner,*
but who is free?

Here I am,
looking at this kernel
of myself,
and I feel
so strangely maternal.
Do I have a choice?
I can't believe I'm hearing

my own mother's voice
giving me advice:

Did you pack your passport?
Sign your traveler's checks?
Don't talk to men,
they only want sex;
keep a ladylike appearance
and when was the last time you sent
a postcard to your parents?

Here it is.
Here's my postcard to me.
I've become my own mother;
never thought I'd be.
But here I am . . .
here I am.

I'VE GOT YOUR PICTURE

HE: I've got your picture,
    it's all I've got,
    and all I've got is remembering
    where I'm not.

    You're in that sunhat—
    I can hardly see
    your face in the shade, but I think
    you're smiling at me.

SHE: I've got your picture,
    it's all I've got
    and all I've got is remembering
    where I'm not.

    In your black T-shirt
    you look so wise.
    The flash made you blink, but who
    could forget those eyes?

SHE: I took only one shot of only you—

HE: I took only one shot of only you—

SHE and HE: And now we're through.

HE: Why did we never ask some innocent
    passerby to take our picture arm in arm?

SHE: We meant to—

  HE: Oh, there were so many things we meant, but

SHE and HE: I never meant to do you any harm.

SHE: I've got your picture,
        it's in a drawer,
        I don't let myself look at it
        anymore.

  HE: No fingerprints,
        it's in a frame.
        I wouldn't let you
        touch it if you came—

SHE and HE: If you only came.

SHE: I've got your picture,
        I don't know why
        but I hope you stare at mine
        and really cry.

  HE: I've got your picture,
        it's deaf and dumb.
        It never calls to tell me
        why you never come.

SHE: It never calls to say why you had to go

HE: I think it's because—

SHE and HE: Because neither of us know.

HE: Hey, I was worth it—

SHE: And so was I—

HE: I've got your picture and—

SHE: I think I understand—

SHE and HE: I love it because it never
says goodbye.

DARK ROOMS

My best friend came back
from his tour of Iraq
a different way than me.

He was lifted off a plane
in a flag-draped coffin
that nobody else could see.

They've got a law to ban
all photos by the press—
to soften all our pain, I guess.

There are dark rooms in my head
like coffins in a row
that nobody will show
'cause nobody wants to know.

Dark rooms like the box
he's buried in. He's dead.
It could have been me instead.

He was just a kid of twenty—
he's not the only one.
Oh, plenty of them to see

in the dark rooms in my head
where I don't want to go.
Why let my feelings show
when nobody wants to know?

He'll never get the chance
to develop or grow
in his dark room in the ground.

There's a governmental ban
on the image of his coffin.
But my buddy was a living man.
Why should he be forgotten?

There are dark rooms in the ground
that no photograph will show,
where soldiers lay their heads.
And nobody wants to know—

Nobody else must know.

IV

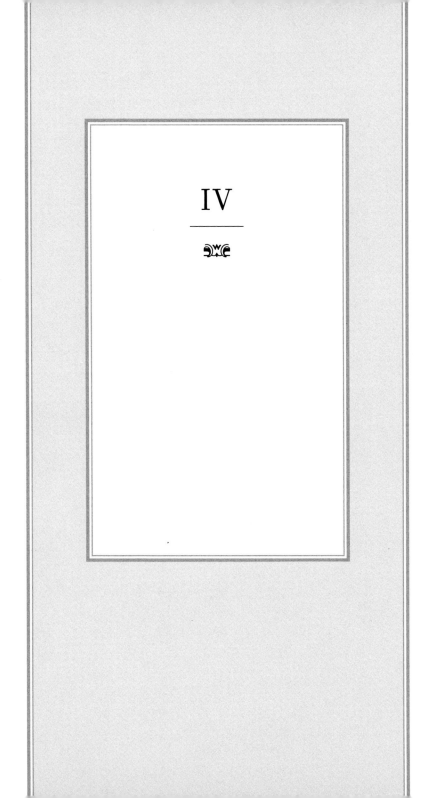

A VANITY TABLE

Mary Jeanne Cassell Cooke, 1929–2014

A few old snapshots, precious, original,
lie scattered artfully for perusal
away from the luncheon table set
along the span of the plate-glass window
in a private room, reserved for its view
across a gorge. The lush and generous
greenness out there seems too primitive
yet to be peopled.

Pictured here, though, from long ago,
is a bride seated at a vanity table.
The forgotten hired photographer
likely asked her to pose like this,
with her silver brush raised stagily
to correct the back of a coiffure
already pinned and sprayed in position.
And the wedding gown was worn by Iris,
her older sister, first.

Still, everything bespeaks her freshness.
Her very slimness seems a form
of the innocence smiling back at her,
the quiet excitement caught in reflection.
Vanity of vanities, all is vanity,
today of all days we should feel it
who have stood by the green plot marked for her

forever; but if truth is what is framed
in a mirror, here was not vanity—

neither in the sense of preening
nor in that of unavailing hope.
Here was simply a glass that faced
an eager, bright unknowingness.
Nothing at all to be confirmed there,
had she sought to learn what awaited her
once she was stepping down the aisle
of years—first the daughter, then a son,
then another, and another one;
their marriages; the grandchildren;
the illnesses, the hurts; the talents
and fulfillments not to be spoken of
too often, or without the soft
laugh she is now remembered for.

No prophecy to be offered either
for the life of her husband, who rises
like a groom now from his central position
at the long, hushed table to speak of her
briefly, modestly. Her final circle
looks up to hear him; looks away and back,
while behind his head a hawk appears
high in the distance, banking its wings
and coasting as it considers something
intently, and almost perfectly,
deep down in the gorge.

SO FAR

All we can say so far
is that we suffer
for nothing.
Not for the self, or
for people at home.
Not for the wisdom.
Not for the love.
Not for the looking
out to the future,
or into the nothing
that goes back so far.

We suffer because
suffering's there.
We hadn't been warned
it got here first,
that it drank all the water
before we were born.
Soon enough we'll join
all the people behind us
who died of thirst
and can tell us nothing
so far.

OLD SAW

The cat is out of the bag,
the horse has left the barn,
the train pulled out of the station,
no bridge is left to burn,
the genie can't be put
back in the bottle, and
in short, it's long been time
to take our medicine.

They threw us under the bus.
It feels as if we're to blame.
Maybe we are: we wonder,
when did we turn obtuse?
How did we lose our charm?
Why do our old saws,
our hats, our radio shows,
so harmless, make them squirm?

And do they think we love
their swearwords and tattoos?
If we could, we'd take a walk.
It's years since we could drive.
They roll their eyes when we talk.
They're glad when we go to bed.
Why did we wake today
on the wrong side of the dead?

DRAPERY FOR GOD THE FATHER

for Mark Leithauser

Wherever I turn, he's already there—
Dürer's determined follower
who has come, like me, to the museum
    to study the masterpieces.

I study him: an old Hells Angel
in damp, unlaundered undershirt
from which pale tufts of armpit hair
    sprout, and make him smell

much as Dürer must have smelled.
He's spellbound by *A Tuft of Cowslips*
(1526, gouache
    on vellum); the blue-gray wash

of *Praying Hands;* the darkening series
of engraver's proofs for Adam and Eve.
Thick as the rhinoceros
    in that woodcut, he stays put—

I skip a room or I backtrack
and yet he blocks me, having swung
into my lane again, a Wild One
    weaving against the traffic.

When he and I were young, I suppose
I could have been the girl behind him

on the Harley, arms around his waist,
   not gaping in distaste

at the rear view of his clothes:
armored as one of Dürer's knights,
his belt is spiked, he's trailing chains
   from the pockets of his jeans,

and sleeving his bare arms, tattoos
by a contemporary artist
were needle-pricked in reds and blues
   that blend now on his skin.

When (a miracle) at last
he steps aside, he leaves me standing
alone before a floating study
   for an altar triptych, lost

in a palace fire two centuries later.
Disembodied twice, then—since
this is *Drapery for God*
   the Father: a priceless heap

of heavy cloth fit for the shape
that moves within it, though unseen.
White hatching, done not with a pen
   but the thinnest paintbrush, brings

forth the weave of light itself.
Dazzling. I look away. And there
he is once more, my heaven-sent
    blind date, my odd opponent

in this afternoon's long scrimmage:
we make eye contact, and agree
wordlessly to share the creator
who made us in his image.

MOON-BREATH

Dark mornings staying dark
longer, another autumn

come, and the body one
day poorer yet,

from restless sleep I wake
early now to note

how the pale disk of moon
caves to its own defeat,

cold as yesterday's fish
left over in the pan,

or miserly as a sliver
of dried soap in a dish.

Oh for a sparkling froth
of cloud, a little heat

from the sun! I shiver
at the window where I plant

one perfect moon-round breath,
as I liked to do as a girl

against the filthy glass
of the yellow school bus

laboring up the hill,
not thinking what I meant

but passionate, as if
I were kissing my own life.

THE BUTTONHOOK

President Roosevelt, touring Ellis Island
in 1906, watched the people from steerage
line up for their six-second physical.

Might not, he wondered aloud, the ungloved handling
of aliens who were ill infect the healthy?
Yet for years more it was done. I imagine

my grandmother, a girl in that Great Hall's
polyglot, reverberating vault
more terrible than church, dazed by the stars

and stripes in the vast banner up in front
where the blessed ones had passed through. Then she did too,
to a room like a little chapel, where her mother

might take Communion. A man in a blue cap
and a blue uniform—a doctor? a policeman?
(Papa would have known, but he had sailed

all alone before them and was waiting
now in New York; yet wasn't this New York?)—
a man in a blue cap reached for her mother.

Without a word (didn't he speak Italian?)
he stuck one finger into her mother's eye,
then turned its lid up with a buttonhook,

the long, curved thing for doing up your boots
when buttons were too many or too small.
You couldn't be American if you were blind

or going to be blind. That much she understood.
She'd go to school, she'd learn to read and write
and teach her parents. The eye man reached to touch

her own face next; she figured she was ready.
She felt big, like that woman in the sea
holding up not a buttonhook but a torch.

LITTLE STAR, 2015

But soon, I'm told, I'll lose my epaulets altogether
and dwindle into a little star.

—JOSEPH BRODSKY, 1940–1996

Joseph, how is your sense of irony
holding up in Heaven?
Did you know, by chance, that the United States
released in 2011

a postage stamp in which your youthful visage
is price-tagged at Forever?
When did you think they'd do that for you in Russia?
How about Never?

Yet here you are, their little star, depicted
in the city you called Peter;
your troubles have been weighed at seventeen rubles
on the poetry meter.

Pressed like a headstrong schoolboy to the corner
of the envelope,
your image puts me in mind of your doting mother,
who never lost hope

she'd see you again (although of course she didn't)
as she stood in line in
the post office, holding a letter to be franked
with the face of Lenin.

A WOMAN'S TALE

In the first scene, I'm eighteen,
with a waist of twenty-four inches.
I'm wearing a sweet blouse
my mother sewed for me.
A businessman in a suit
comes walking down the street,
stops in his tracks, and cries,
"My God, you're adorable.
I want you to have my babies!"
Then, good-naturedly
shaking his head, not waiting
for any sort of reply—
and what on earth would I say?—
he keeps on ambulating.

A decade later. Another
man has found me winning:
this one impregnates me.
We'd done the romantic thing,
the ring, the honeymoon.
Now, on a scorching day
in July, some guy approaching
on the sidewalk takes me in:
at nine months gone, five-three,
I'm nothing but a belly

waddling along like Falstaff.
He flings his head back to laugh—
a belly laugh, if you will.

That was thirty summers ago,
and it still gives me a chill.

LO SPOSALIZIO

That's the shorthand for it,
The Marriage of the Virgin
stuffed here in my pocket—

a masterpiece in soft
washable microfiber,
a cloth six inches square

designed to clean the lenses
on fingerprinted glasses
and reproduce the clear

triumph of the rational
(oil on poplar panel)
in the ceremony Raphael

composed for Mary and Joseph.
Their modest heads incline
to harmonize, as if

half-note ovals penned
on a staff made by the patterned
stones in the piazza—

geometries that bend
to a vanishing point beyond
a Romanesque, domed temple

porticoed with arches
along its base, except for
(far off) a rectangular

door that gives on air,
blue hills and air, the future
until it is the past.

Perspective and proportion
are what the bearded priest
is authorized to join

as he guides the husband's wrist
to place the ring on a destined
finger on her hand.

Yet every head's its own.
The congregation's faces
turn against symmetries,

gaze this way or that
or inward, while a number
of background figures whisper

like stands of distant trees.
Even the draperies
(the gold cloak falling from

the bridegroom's emerald shoulder;
her mantle's swag of sapphire
wrapping the ruby gown)

assert, for all their mass
and balance, how the fabric
of the moment improvises

and unfolds as it will.
Such, now, is the time in
which you, my new son Simon,

stand in your bow tie;
you, Emily, the child
I swaddled once, are veiled

as only brides may be.
Now may the mystery start.
With nothing to espouse

but hope as old as art,
I clutch the little cloth
in case need should arise

to wipe my naked eyes.

THE HOTEL BELVEDERE

A June day under the Jungfrau.
Near the railway that brought her here,
an old woman sits on a bench.
She isn't facing the Jungfrau
but the Hotel Belvedere

which has, as its name implies,
a beautiful view of the Jungfrau,
a name for what she had been
when she last saw it, maybe,
on her honeymoon.

She regards the hotel intently,
studies what I assume
were the windows of their room.
Was it hard to come back alone,
hobbling on that cane?

No, not alone: her husband
and daughter (or granddaughter—
surely this couple's offspring
can't be very young)
have arrived with ice cream cones,

inverted mountains where snow
is piled on the widest end.
They make the most of that pleasure
before, like a magic trick,
a tripod's pulled from a backpack.

Steady as you go
is what the granddaughter says
as she pulls the old woman up
and the three of them, like a tripod,
lean to make one shape

that peaks on top, like the Jungfrau.
But the hotel's the backdrop.
The camera's timed to snap
at a smile, and another smile;
new pose, and it snaps again.

Even the staring stranger
who has no need to invent
their story is distracted
from the majesty of the Jungfrau,
and heeding gestures meant

to yield up little grandeur:
the acts of a granddaughter
who, when she's old, will tell
of the long journey they took
back to the hotel,

the origin of what mattered
to a few vanished people.
There was ice cream; and a view
of the snowcapped Jungfrau,
which is nowhere pictured.

AN AFGHAN CARPET

Bring me just notice of the numbers dead
On both our parts.

—*HENRY V*

Centuries of illiterate
women, think of it, making them one by one
on portable looms, knotting the fringes by hand,
delineating along the way
the figured border, the either-or,

between home ground and what's beyond
the raveled shore;
between us and anonymous
landlocked nomads in their tents.

What is this carpet's provenance?
Herati pattern. Made in Afghanistan.
Purchased years ago in Bahrain
in a little shop where
the chatty proprietor served tea;
then given to me

by you, my beloved, that scared-as-hell
young man from Indiana, churchy
and virtuous, who got to finish college
before your number was up.
You too would come to sleep in tents;
you dressed and spoke in camouflage,
handpicked for Intelligence.

Clueless, I consult a map
for what hems Afghanistan in.
Turkmenistan, China, Pakistan,
Uzbekistan, Iran . . .
the cartographer's inked
lines in the sand,
named-and-renamed
infringements.

Think of the line
of elephants, as grand as time,
thundering over the Hindu Kush
repeatedly in these octagons
that stand for their giant prints.
Motifs that stomp
the margins like a postmaster's stamp
over and over, he cannot stop,
on the carpet's envelope.

Art as target. Art as grid
where secret combatants are hidden.
Prayer rug whose standard size
is a village square.
What do I know?
Nothing. But I hear it underfoot:
the terrible, low
warble of warplanes.

And sometimes I see five miles high
an enemy, silent, without a face
in uncontested airspace,
dropping ordnance from a leather chair
in (can it be?) Las Vegas.

Move in with me. This is our house.
This will be us:
first, we'll get to be alive.
And then we'll have
labor-saving appliances,
megatons of mail-ordered stuff,
an Afghan carpet, a smart TV
larger than good taste might warrant
but face it, our eyes
are no longer what they were.

Let's sit above this homemade, nomad
carpet woven by women
in black shapes on fields of red.
The spade-shapes look like missiles.
The one-armed shapes like jugs
seem they might put out flames.

Each of us in a leather chair
and primed, with a glass of wine, for tonight's
mystery set in some English hamlet

where a murder is solved every week,
let's confess: we can't
unearth the carpeted names.

Acknowledgments

Thanks to the editors of the journals where these poems appeared, sometimes in slightly different form.

Ambit: "The Surveyors"

The American Scholar: "Aloe," "Mr. Boyfriend," "So Far"

The Antioch Review: "Dragnet," "Tennis in the Snow"

The Common: "Bratislava," "Here I Am," "The Hotel Belvedere," "We'll Always Have Parents"

The Fiddlehead: "Little Men," "Moon-Breath," "A Vanity Table"

The Hopkins Review: "St. Florian with Burning Church"

Little Star: "Little Star, 2015," "Vierge Ouvrante"

National Archives (www.archives.gov) and poets.org: "The Buttonhook"

Plume: "Advantage Federer," "A Word from Our Sponsor"

Poetry Northwest: "Lo Sposalizio," "Old Saw"

Southwest Review: "An Afghan Carpet," "Today's Specials"

Women's Studies Quarterly: "A Woman's Tale"

The Yale Review: "The Bickers," "Drapery for God the Father," "Pastry Level," "The Profane Piano Tuner," "Smoking the Dead Sea Scrolls"

Mary Jo Salter is the author of seven previous poetry collections and a children's book. She has been a coeditor of *The Norton Anthology of Poetry* in various editions since 1996. As the Krieger-Eisenhower Professor in The Writing Seminars at Johns Hopkins University, she lives in Baltimore.

A NOTE ABOUT THE TYPE

Pierre Simon Fournier le jeune (1712–1768), who designed the type used in this book, was both an originator and a collector of types. His services to the art of printing were his design of letters, his creation of ornaments and initials, and his standardization of type sizes. His types are old style in character and sharply cut. In 1764 and 1766 he published his *Manuel typographique*, a treatise on the history of French types and printing, on typefounding in all its details, and on what many consider his most important contribution to typography—the measurement of type by the point system.

COMPOSED BY NORTH MARKET STREET GRAPHICS,
LANCASTER, PENNSYLVANIA

PRINTED AND BOUND BY BERRYVILLE GRAPHICS,
BERRYVILLE, VIRGINIA

DESIGNED BY BETTY LEW